THE GREAT FAIRY TALE SEARCH

There are things to spot in every scene in this magical book – from Cinderella's lost slipper to Aladdin's magic lamp. If you get stuck, all the answers are in the back.

I'm also hidden in every scene – can you find me?

Illustrated by Chuck Whelon

Edited by Hannah Cohen

Buster Books

Little Red Riding Hood

1 Little Red Riding Hood

1 daffodil

1 basket

1 nest

1 strawberry plant

5 toadstools

1 bear

4 orange butterflies

7 acorns

1 Big Bad Wolf

2 deer

Cinderella

1 Prince

6 footmen

1 Wicked Stepmother

1 glass slipper

6 mice

3 pumpkins

Cinderella

1

Fairy Godmother

1

Ugly Sisters

2

4 bats

1 clock

The Little Mermaid

1 Sea King

7 seahorses

1 oyster shell and pearl

1 red and yellow fish

3 starfish

1 anchor

1 dolphin

1 weeping willow tree

1 marble statue

5 jellyfish

1 Little Mermaid

Snow White

1 Snow White

7 dwarves

3 squirrels

1 roast chicken

7 pickaxes

7 little loaves of bread

1 Wicked Witch

1 little lamps

7 little lamps

1 red robin

2 rabbits

1 big spotty pot

Sleeping Beauty

1 Kind Fairy

3 sleeping violinists

1 Wicked Fairy

1 golden eagle

1 Sleeping Beauty

2 sleeping dogs

1 Prince

5 sleeping guards

1 sleeping Queen

1 sleeping King

1 spinning wheel

The Princess and the Pea

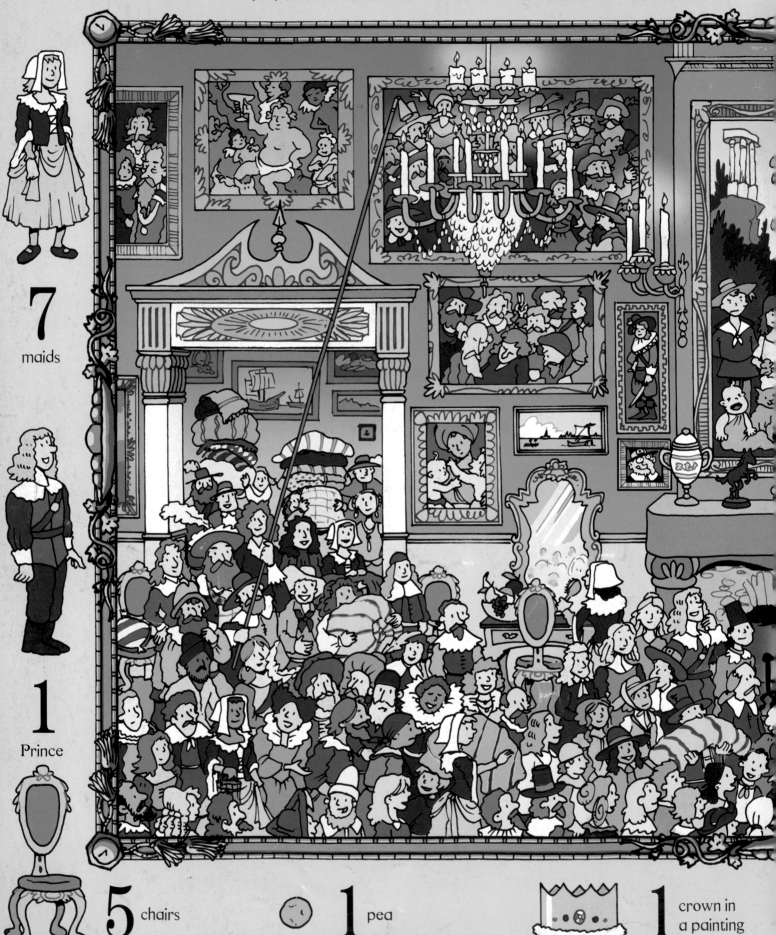

7 maids

1 Prince

5 chairs

1 pea

1 crown in a painting

1 snow-white bird

10 candy canes

5 brown gingerbread men

1 Witch

3 mallard ducks

2 rabbits

1 wishing well

The Pied Piper of Hamelin

2 wheelbarrows

1 cat and her kittens

1 man falling off a ladder

1 woman sweeping

1 basket of laundry

2 children dancing

1 rat on a washing line

1
Genie

1
Princess
Badroulbadour

5 bats

1 lamp

1 ruby tiara

4 sapphire goblets

1 Aladdin

1 jewelled necklace

1 chest of gold coins

1 golden camel

The Frog Prince

1 golden ball

1 Queen

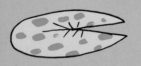
3 spotty lily pads

4 dragonflies

 **3** mallard ducks

 **5** rose bushes

1 golden boy fountain

1 Princess

 **6** pond snails

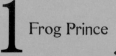 **1** dog

1 Frog Prince

Jack and the Beanstalk

1 Jack

1 Jack's Mother

1 Daisy the cow

10 gold coins

3 sheep

5 snakes

1 gold harp

1 Giant

1 axe

3 ladybirds

1 hen with a golden egg

Pinocchio

1 Jack-in-the-box

1 Pinocchio

1 wooden doll

2 pairs of wooden clogs

5 hammers

4 jars of paint

1 Geppetto

1 cuckoo clock

1 wind-up ballerina

3 spinning tops

1 sly fox and cat

1 rocking horse

Answers

Cinderella

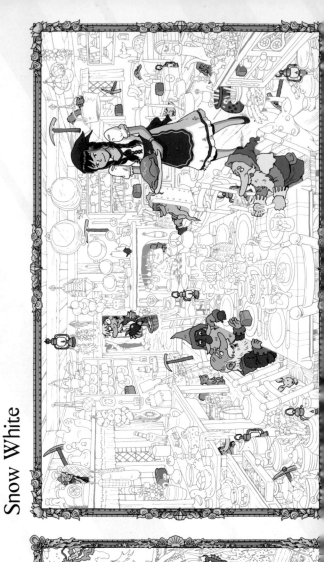

Snow White

Little Red Riding Hood

The Little Mermaid

The Princess and the Pea

The Princess and the Pea

The Pied Piper of Hamelin

Sleeping Beauty

Hansel and Gretel

Answers

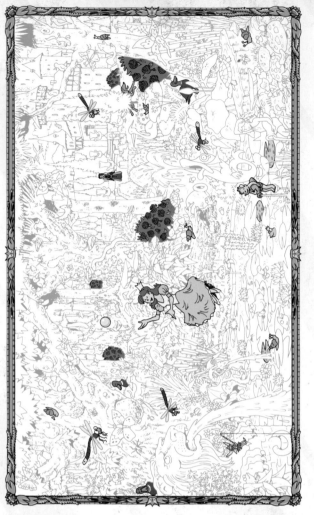

The Frog Prince

Pinocchio

The Adventures of Aladdin

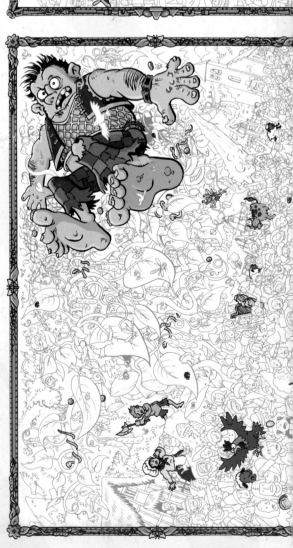

Jack and the Beanstalk